Christopher Columbus
And The New World of His Discovery
Volume 4

Filson Young

[ZHINGOORA BOOKS]

This edition is published by
Zhingoora Books.

About Author

Alexander Bell Filson Young was a journalist, BBC programme advisor and author. His wrote the book on Titanic, a RMS Titanic ship. His famous works includeTitanic, The Relief of Mafekingand etc.

CHAPTER IV

THE HOUR OF TRIUMPH

From the moment when Columbus set foot on Spanish soil in the spring of 1493 he was surrounded by a fame and glory which, although they were transient, were of a splendour such as few other men can have ever experienced. He had not merely discovered a country, he had discovered a world. He had not merely made a profitable expedition; he had brought the promise of untold wealth to the kingdom of Spain. He had not merely made himself the master of savage tribes; he had conquered the supernatural, and overcome for ever those powers of darkness that had been thought to brood over the vast Atlantic. He had sailed away in obscurity, he had returned in fame; he had departed under a cloud of scepticism and ridicule, he had come again in power and glory. He had sailed from Palos as a seeker after hidden wealth, hidden knowledge; he returned as teacher, discoverer, benefactor. The whole of Spain rang with his fame, and the echoes of it spread to Portugal, France, England, Germany, and Italy; and it reached the ears of his own family, who had now left the Vico Dritto di Ponticello in Genoa and were living at Savona.

His life ashore in the first weeks following his return was a succession of triumphs and ceremonials. His first care on landing had been to go with the whole of his crew to the church of Saint George, where a Te Deum was sung in honour of his return; and afterwards to perform those vows that he had made at sea in the hour of danger. There was a certain amount of business to transact at Palos in connection with the paying of the ships' crews, writing of reports to the Sovereigns, and so forth; and it is likely that he stayed with his friends at the monastery of La Rabida while this was being done. The Court was at Barcelona; and it was probably only a sense of his own great dignity and importance that prevented Christopher from setting off on the long journey immediately. But he who had made so many pilgrimages to Court as a suitor could revel in a position that made it possible for him to hang back, and to be pressed and invited; and so when his business at Palos was finished he sent a messenger with his letters and reports to Barcelona, and himself, with his crew and his Indians and all his trophies, departed for Seville, where he arrived on Palm Sunday.

His entrance into that city was only a foretaste of the glory in which he was to move across the whole of Spain. He was met at the gates of the city by a squadron of cavalry commanded by an envoy sent by Queen Isabella; and a procession was formed of members of the crew carrying parrots, alive and stuffed, fruits, vegetables, and various other products of the New World.

In a prominent place came the Indians, or rather four of them, for one had died on the day they entered Palos and three were too ill to leave that town; but the ones that took part in the procession got all the more attention and admiration. The streets of Seville were crowded; crowded also were the windows, balconies, and roofs. The Admiral was entertained at the house of the Count of Cifuentes, where his little museum of dead and live curiosities was also accommodated, and where certain favoured visitors were admitted to view it. His two sons, Diego and Ferdinand, were sent from Cordova to join him; and perhaps he found time to visit Beatriz, although there is no record of his having been to Cordova or of her having come to Seville.

Meanwhile his letters and messengers to the King and Queen had produced their due effect. The almost incredible had come to pass, and they saw themselves the monarchs not merely of Spain, but of a new Empire that might be as vast as Europe and Africa together. On the 30th of March they despatched a special messenger with a letter to Columbus, whose eyes must have sparkled and heart expanded when he read the superscription: "From the King and Queen to Don Christoval Colon, their Admiral of the Ocean Seas and Viceroy and Governor of the Islands discovered in the Indies." No lack of titles and dignities now! Their Majesties express a profound sense of his ability and distinction, of the greatness of his services to them, to the Church, and to God Himself. They hope that he will lose no time, but repair to Barcelona immediately, so that they can have the pleasure of hearing from his own lips an account of his wonderful expedition, and of discussing with him the preparations that must immediately be set on foot to fit out a new one. On receiving this letter Christopher immediately drew up a list of what he thought necessary for the new expedition and, collecting all his retinue and his museum of specimens, started by road for Barcelona.

Every one in Spain had by this time heard more or less exaggerated accounts of the discoveries, and the excitement in the towns and villages through which he passed was extreme. Wherever he went he was greeted and feasted like a king returning from victorious wars; the people lined the streets of the towns and villages, and hung out banners, and gazed their fill at the Indians and at the strange sun-burned faces of the crew. At Barcelona, where they arrived towards the end of April, the climax of these glittering dignities was reached. When the King and Queen heard that Columbus was approaching the town they had their throne prepared under a magnificent pavilion, and in the hot sunshine of that April day they sat and waited the—coming of the great man. A glittering troop of cavalry had been sent out to meet him, and at the gates of the town a procession was formed similar to that at Seville. He had now six natives with him, who occupied an important place in the procession;

sailors also, who carried baskets of fruit and vegetables from Espanola, with stuffed birds and animals, and a monstrous lizard held aloft on a stick. The Indians were duly decked out in all their paint and feathers; but if they were a wonder and marvel to the people of Spain, what must Spain have been to them with its great buildings and cities, its carriages and horses, its glittering dresses and armours, its splendour and luxury! We have no record of what the Indians thought, only of what the crowd thought who gaped upon them and upon the gaudy parrots that screeched and fluttered also in the procession. Columbus came riding on horseback, as befitted a great Admiral and Viceroy, surrounded by his pilots and principal officers; and followed by men bearing golden belts, golden masks, nuggets of gold and dust of gold, and preceded by heralds, pursuivants, and mace-bearers.

What a return for the man who three years before had been pointed at and laughed to scorn in this same brilliant society! The crowds pressed so closely that the procession could hardly get through the streets; the whole population was there to witness it; and the windows and balconies and roofs of the houses, as well as the streets themselves, were thronged with a gaily dressed and wildly excited crowd. At length the procession reaches the presence of the King and Queen and, crowning and unprecedented honour! as the Admiral comes before them Ferdinand and Isabella rise to greet him. Under their own royal canopy a seat is waiting for him; and when he has made his ceremonial greeting he is invited to sit in their presence and give an account of his voyage.

He is fully equal to the situation; settles down to do himself and his subject justice; begins, we may be sure, with a preamble about the providence of God and its wisdom and consistency in preserving the narrator and preparing his life for this great deed; putting in a deal of scientific talk which had in truth nothing to do with the event, but was always applied to it in Columbus's writings from this date onwards; and going on to describe the voyage, the sea of weeds, the landfall, his intercourse with the natives, their aptitude for labour and Christianity, and the hopes he has of their early conversion to the Catholic Church. And then follows a long description of the wonderful climate, "like May in Andalusia," the noble rivers, and gorgeous scenery, the trees and fruits and flowers and singing birds; the spices and the cotton; and chief of all, the vast stores of gold and pearls of which the Admiral had brought home specimens. At various stages in his narrative he produces illustrations; now a root of rhubarb or allspice; now a raw nugget of gold; now a piece of gold laboured into a mask or belt; now a native decorated with the barbaric ornaments that were the fashion in Espanola. These things, says Columbus, are mere first-fruits of the harvest that is to come; the things which he, like the dove that had flown across the sea from the Ark and brought back an olive leaf in its mouth, has brought back across the stormy seas to that Ark of civilisation from which he had flown forth.

It was to Columbus an opportunity of stretching his visionary wings and creating with pompous words and images a great halo round himself of dignity and wonder and divine distinction,—an opportunity such as he loved, and such as he never failed to make use of.

The Sovereigns were delighted and profoundly impressed. Columbus wound up his address with an eloquent peroration concerning the glory to Christendom of these new discoveries; and there followed an impressive silence, during which the Sovereigns sank on their knees and raised hands and tearful eyes to heaven, an example in which they were followed by the whole of the assembly; and an appropriate gesture enough, seeing what was to come of it all. The choir of the Chapel Royal sang a solemn Te Deum on the spot; and the Sovereigns and nobles, bishops, archbishops, grandees, hidalgos, chamberlains, treasurers, chancellors and other courtiers, being exhausted by these emotions, retired to dinner.

During his stay at Barcelona Columbus was the guest of the Cardinal-Archbishop of Toledo, and moved thus in an atmosphere of combined temporal and spiritual dignity such as his soul loved. Very agreeable indeed to him was the honour shown to him at this time. Deep down in his heart there was a secret nerve of pride and vanity which throughout his life hitherto had been continually mortified and wounded; but he was able now to indulge his appetite for outward pomp and honour as much as he pleased. When King Ferdinand went out to ride Columbus would be seen riding on one side of him, the young Prince John riding on the other side; and everywhere, when he moved among the respectful and admiring throng, his grave face was seen to be wreathed in complacent smiles. His hair, which had turned white soon after he was thirty, gave him a dignified and almost venerable appearance, although he was only in his forty-third year; and combined with his handsome and commanding presence to excite immense enthusiasm among the Spaniards. They forgot for the moment what they had formerly remembered and were to remember again—that he was a foreigner, an Italian, a man of no family and of poor origin. They saw in him the figure-head of a new empire and a new glory, an emblem of power and riches, of the dominion which their proud souls loved; and so there beamed upon him the brief fickle sunshine of their smiles and favour, which he in his delusion regarded as an earnest of their permanent honour and esteem.

It is almost always thus with a man not born to such dignities, and who comes by them through his own efforts and labours. No one would grudge him the short-lived happiness of these summer weeks; but although he believed himself to be as happy as a man can be, he appears to quietly contemplating eyes less happy and fortunate than when he stood alone on the deck of his ship, surrounded by an untrustworthy crew, prevailing by his own unaided efforts over the difficulties and dangers with which he was surrounded. Court functions and processions, and the companionship of kings and cardinals, are indeed no suitable reward for the kind of work that he did. Courtly dignities are suited to courtly services; but they are no suitable crown for rough labour and hardship at sea, or for the fulfilment of a man's self by lights within him; no suitable crown for any solitary labour whatsoever, which must always be its own and only reward.

It is to this period of splendour that the story of the egg, which is to some people the only familiar incident in Columbian biography, is attributed. The story is that at a banquet given by the Cardinal-Arch bishop the conversation ran, as it always did in those days when he was present, on the subject of the Admiral's discoveries; and that one of the guests remarked that it was all very well for Columbus to have done what he did, but that in a country like Spain, where there were so many men learned in science and cosmography, and many able mariners besides, some one else would certainly have been found who would have done the same thing. Whereupon Columbus, calling for an egg, laid a wager that none of the company but him self could make it stand on its end without support. The egg was brought and passed round, and every one tried to make it stand on end, but without success. When it came to Columbus he cracked the shell at one end, making a flat surface on which the egg stood upright; thus demonstrating that a thing might be wonderful, not because it was difficult or impossible, but merely because no one had ever thought of doing it before. A sufficiently inane story, and by no means certainly true; but there is enough character in this little feat, ponderous, deliberate, pompous, ostentatious, and at bottom a trick and deceitful quibble, to make it accord with the grandiloquent public manner of Columbus, and to make it easily believable of one who chose to show himself in his speech and writings so much more meanly and pretentiously than he showed himself in the true acts and business of his life.

But pomp and parade were not the only occupation of these Barcelona days. There were long consultations with Ferdinand and Isabella about the colonisation of the new lands; there were intrigues, and parrying of intrigues, between the Spanish and Portuguese Courts on the subject of the discoveries and of the representative rights of the two nations to be the religious saviours of the New World. The Pope, to whose hands the heathen were entrusted by God to be handed for an inheritance to the highest and most religious bidder, had at that time innocently divided them into two portions, to wit: heathen to the south of Spain and Portugal, and heathen to the west of those places. By the Bull of 1438, granted by Pope Martin V., the heathen to the west had been given to the Spanish, and the heathen to the south to the Portuguese, and the two crowns had in 1479 come to a working agreement. Now, however, the existence of more heathen to the west of the Azores introduced a new complication, and Ferdinand sent a message to Pope Alexander VI. praying for a confirmation of the Spanish title to the new discoveries.

This Pope, who was a native of Aragon and had been a subject of Ferdinand, was a stolid, perverse, and stubborn being; so much is advertised in his low forehead, impudent prominent nose, thick sensual lips, and stout bull neck. This Pope considers the matter; considers, by such lights as he has, to whom he shall entrust the souls of these new heathen; considers which country, Spain or Portugal, is most likely to hold and use the same for the increase of the Christian faith in general, the furtherance of the Holy Catholic Church in special, and the aggrandisement of Popes in particular; and shrewdly decides that the country in which the. Inquisition can flourish is the country to whom the heathen souls should be entrusted. He therefore issues a Bull, dated May 3, 1493, granting to the Spanish the possession of all lands, not occupied by Christian powers, that lie west of a meridian drawn one hundred leagues to the westward of the Azores, and to the Portuguese possession of all similar lands lying to the eastward of that line. He sleeps upon this Bull, and has inspiration; and on the morrow, May 4th, issues another Bull, drawing a line from the arctic to the antarctic pole, and granting to Spain all heathen inheritance to the westward of the same. The Pope, having signed this Bull, considers it further-assisted, no doubt, by the Portuguese Ambassador at the Vatican, to whom it has been shown; realises that in the wording of the Bull an injustice has been done to Portugal, since Spain is allowed to fix very much at her own convenience the point at which the line drawn from pole to pole shall cut the equator; and also because, although Spain is given all the lands in existence within her territory, Portugal is only given the lands which she may actually have occupied. Even the legal mind of the Pope, although much drowsed and blunted by brutish excesses, discerns faultiness in this document; and consequently on the same day issues a third Bull, in which the injustice to Portugal is redressed. Nothing so easy, thinks the Pope, as to issue Bulls; if you make a mistake in one Bull, issue another; and, having issued three Bulls in twenty-four hours, he desists for the present, having divided the earthly globe.

Thus easy it is for a Pope to draw lines from pole to pole, and across the deep of the sea. Yet the poles sleep still in their icy virginal sanctity, and the blue waves through which that papal line passes shift and shimmer and roll in their free salt loneliness, unaffected by his demarcation; the heathen also, it appears, since that distant day, have had something to say to their disposition. If he had slept upon it another night, poor Pope, it might have occurred to him that west and east might meet on a meridian situated elsewhere on the globe than one hundred miles west of the Azores; and that the Portuguese, who for the moment had nothing heathen except Africa left to them, might according to his demarcation strike a still richer vein of heathendom than that granted to Spain. But the holy Pontiff, bull neck, low forehead, impudent prominent nose, and sensual lips notwithstanding, is exhausted by his cosmographical efforts, and he lets it rest at that. Later, when Spain discovers that her privileges have been abated, he will have to issue another Bull; but not to-day. Sufficient unto the day are the Bulls thereof. For the moment King proposes and Pope disposes; but the matter lies ultimately in the hands of the two eternal protagonists, man and God.

In the meantime here are six heathen alive and well, or at any rate well enough to support, willy-nilly, the rite of holy baptism. They must have been sufficiently dazed and bewildered by all that had happened to them since they were taken on board the Admiral's ship, and God alone knows what they thought of it all, or whether they thought anything more than the parrots that screamed and fluttered and winked circular eyes in the procession with them. Doubtless they were willing enough; and indeed, after all they had come through, a little cold water could not do them any harm. So baptized they were in Barcelona; pompously baptized with infinite state and ceremony, the King and Queen and Prince Juan officiating as sponsors. Queen Isabella, after the manner of queens, took a kindly feminine interest in these heathen, and in their brethren across the sea. She had seen a good deal of conquest, and knew her Spaniard pretty intimately; and doubtless her maternal heart had some misgivings about the ultimate happiness of the gentle, handsome creatures who lived in the sunshine in that distant place. She made their souls her especial care, and honestly believed that by providing for their spiritual conversion she was doing them the greatest service in her power. She provided from her own private chapel vestments and altar furniture for the mission church in Espanola; she had the six exiles in Barcelona instructed under her eye; and she gave Columbus special orders to inflict severe punishments on any one who should offer the natives violence or injustice of any kind. It must be remembered to her credit that in after days, when slavery and an intolerable bloody and brutish oppression had turned the paradise of Espanola into a shambles, she fought almost singlehanded, and with an ethical sense far in advance of her day, against the system of slavery practised by Spain upon the inhabitants of the New World.

The dignities that had been provisionally granted to Columbus before his departure on the first voyage were now elaborately confirmed; and in addition he was given another title—that of Captain-General of the large fleet which was to be fitted out to sail to the new colonies. He was entrusted with the royal seal, which gave him the right to grant letters patent, to issue commissions, and to Appoint deputies in the royal name. A coat-of-arms was also granted to him in which, in its original form, the lion and castle of Leon and Castile were quartered with islands of the sea or on a field azure, and five anchors or on a field azure. This was changed from time to time, chiefly by Columbus himself, who afterwards added a continent to the islands, and modified the blazonry of the lion and castle to agree with those on the royal arms—a piece of ignorance and childish arrogance which was quite characteristic of him.

> [A motto has since been associated with the coat-of-arms, although
> it is not certain that Columbus adopted it in his lifetime. In one
> form it reads:
> > "Por Castilla e por Leon
> > Nueva Mundo hallo Colon."]

(For Castile and Leon Columbus found a New World.)

And in the other:

> "A Castilla y a Leon
> Nuevo Mundo dio Colon."

(To Castile and Leon Columbus gave a New World.)

Equally characteristic and less excusable was his acceptance of the pension of ten thousand maravedis which had been offered to the member of the expedition who should first sight land. Columbus was granted a very large gratuity on his arrival in Barcelona, and even taking the product of the islands at a tenth part of their value as estimated by him, he still had every right to suppose himself one of the richest men in Spain. Yet he accepted this paltry pension of L8. 6s. 8d. in our modern money (of 1900), which, taking the increase in the purchasing power of money at an extreme estimate, would not be more than the equivalent of $4000 now. Now Columbus had not been the first person to see land; he saw the light, but it was Rodrigo de Triana, the look-out man on the Pinta, who first saw the actual land. Columbus in his narrative to the King and Queen would be sure to make much of the seeing of the light, and not so much of the actual sighting of land; and he was on the spot, and the reward was granted to him. Even if we assume that in strict equity Columbus was entitled to it, it was at least a matter capable of argument, if only Rodrigo de Triana had been there to argue it; and what are we to think of the Admiral of the Ocean Seas and Viceroy of the Indies who thus takes what can only be called a mean advantage of a poor seaman in his employ? It would have been a competence and a snug little fortune to Rodrigo de Triana; it was a mere flea-bite to a man who was thinking in eighth parts of continents. It may be true, as Oviedo alleges, that Columbus transferred it to Beatriz Enriquez; but he had no right to provide for her out of money that in all equity and decency ought to have gone to another and a poorer man. His biographers, some of whom have vied with his canonisers in insisting upon seeing virtue in his every action, have gone to all kinds of ridiculous extremes in accounting for this piece of meanness. Irving says that it was "a subject in which his whole ambition was involved"; but a plain person will regard it as an instance of greed and love of money. We must not shirk facts like this if we wish to know the man as he really was. That he was capable of kindness and generosity, and that he was in the main kind-hearted, we have fortunately no reason to doubt; and if I dwell on some of his less amiable characteristics it is with no desire to magnify them out of their due proportion. They are part of that side of him that lay in shadow, as some side of each one of us lies; for not all by light nor all by shade, but by light and shade combined, is the image of a man made visible to us.

It is quite of a piece with the character of Columbus that while he was writing a receipt for the look-out man's money and thinking what a pretty gift it would make for Beatriz Enriquez he was planning a splendid and spectacular thank-offering for all the dignities to which he had been raised; and, brooding upon the vast wealth that was now to be his, that he should register a vow to furnish within seven years an expedition of four thousand horse and fifty thousand foot for the rescue of the Holy Sepulchre, and a similar force within five years after the first if it should be necessary. It was probable that the vow was a provisional one, and that its performance was to be contingent on his actual receipt and possession of the expected money; for as we know, there was no money and no expedition. The vow was in effect a kind of religious flourish much beloved by Columbus, undertaken seriously and piously enough, but belonging rather to his public than to his private side. A much more simple and truly pious act of his was, not the promising of visionary but the sending of actual money to his old father in Savona, which he did immediately after his arrival in Spain. The letter which he wrote with that kindly remittance, not being couched in the pompous terms which he thought suitable for princes, and doubtless giving a brief homely account of what he had done, would, if we could come by it, be a document beyond all price; but like every other record of his family life it has utterly perished.

He wrote also from Barcelona to his two brothers, Bartholomew and Giacomo, or James, since we may as well give him the English equivalent of his name. Bartholomew was in France, whither he had gone some time after his return from his memorable voyage with Bartholomew Diaz; he was employed as a map-maker at the court of Anne de Beaujeu, who was reigning in the temporary absence of her brother Charles VIII. Columbus's letter reached him, but much too late for him to be able to join in the second expedition; in fact he did not reach Seville until five months after it had sailed. James, however, who was now twenty-five years old, was still at Savona; he, like Columbus, had been apprenticed to his father, but had apparently remained at home earning his living either as a wool-weaver or merchant. He was a quiet, discreet young fellow, who never pushed himself forward very much, wore very plain clothes, and was apparently much overawed by the grandeur and dignity of his elder brother. He was, however, given a responsible post in the new expedition, and soon had his fill of adventure.

The business of preparing for the new expedition was now put in hand, and Columbus, having taken leave of Ferdinand and Isabella, went to Seville to superintend the preparations. All the ports in Andalusia were ordered to supply such vessels as might be required at a reasonable cost, and the old order empowering the Admiral to press mariners into the service was renewed. But this time it was unnecessary; the difficulty now was rather to keep down the number of applicants for berths in the expedition, and to select from among the crowd of adventurers who offered themselves those most suitable for the purposes of the new colony. In this work Columbus was assisted by a commissioner whom the Sovereigns had appointed to superintend the fitting out of the expedition. This man was a cleric, Juan Rodriguez de Fonseca, Archdeacon of Seville, a person of excellent family and doubtless of high piety, and of a surpassing shrewdness for this work. He was of a type very commonly produced in Spain at this period; a very able organiser, crafty and competent, but not altogether trustworthy on a point of honour. Like so many ecclesiastics of this stamp, he lived for as much power and influence as he could achieve; and though he was afterwards bishop of three sees successively, and became Patriarch of the Indies, he never let go his hold on temporal affairs. He began by being jealous of Columbus, and by objecting to the personal retinue demanded by the Admiral; and in this, if I know anything of the Admiral, he was probably justified. The matter was referred to the Sovereigns, who ordered Fonseca to carry out the

Admiral's wishes; and the two were immediately at loggerheads. When the Council for the Indies was afterwards formed Fonseca became head, of it, and had much power to make things pleasant or otherwise for Columbus.

It became necessary now to raise a considerable sum of money for the new expedition. Two-thirds of the ecclesiastical tithes were appropriated, and a large proportion of the confiscated property of the Jews who had been banished from Spain the year before; but this was not enough; and five million maravedis were borrowed from the Duke of Medina Sidonia in order to complete the financial supplies necessary for this very costly expedition. There was a treasurer, Francisco Pinelo, and an accountant, Juan de Soria, who had charge of all the financial arrangements; but the whole of the preparations were conducted on a ruinously expensive scale, owing to the haste which the diplomatic relations with Portugal made necessary. The provisioning was done by a Florentine merchant named Juonato Beradi, who had an assistant named Amerigo Vespucci—who, by a strange accident, was afterwards to give his name to the continent of the New World.

While these preparations were going on the game of diplomacy was being played between the Courts of Spain and Portugal. King John of Portugal had the misfortune to be badly advised; and he was persuaded that, although he had lost the right to the New World through his rejection of Columbus's services when they were first offered to him, he might still discover it for himself, relying for protection on the vague wording of the papal Bulls. He immediately began to prepare a fleet, nominally to go to the coast of Africa, but really to visit the newly discovered lands in the west. Hearing of these preparations, King Ferdinand sent an Ambassador to the Portuguese Court; and King John agreed also to appoint an Ambassador to discuss the whole matter of the line of demarcation, and in the meantime not to allow any of his ships to sail to the west for a period of sixty days after his Ambassador had reached Barcelona. There followed a good deal of diplomatic sharp practice; the Portuguese bribing the Spanish officials to give them information as to what was going on, and the Spaniards furnishing their envoys with double sets of letters and documents so that they could be prepared to counter any movement on the part of King John. The idea of the Portuguese was that the line of demarcation should be a parallel rather than a meridian; and that everything north of the Canaries should belong to Spain and everything south to Portugal; but this would never do from the Spanish point of view. The fact that a proposal had come from Portugal, however, gave Ferdinand an opportunity of delaying the diplomatic proceedings until his own expedition was actually ready to set sail; and he wrote to Columbus repeatedly, urging him to make all possible haste with his preparations. In the meantime he despatched a solemn embassy to Portugal, the purport of which, much beclouded and delayed by preliminary and impossible proposals, was to submit the whole question to the Pope for arbitration. And all the time he was busy petitioning the Pope to restore to Spain those concessions granted in the second Bull, but taken away again in the third.

This, being much egged on to it, the Pope ultimately did; waking up on September 26th, the day after Columbus's departure, and issuing another Bull in which the Spanish Sovereigns were given all lands and islands, discovered or not discovered, which might be found by sailing west and south. Four Bulls; and after puzzling over them for a year, the Kings of Spain and Portugal decided to make their own Bull, and abide by it, which, having appointed commissioners, they did on June 7, 1494., when by the Treaty of Tordecillas the line of demarcation was finally fixed to pass from north to south through a point 370 leagues west of the Cape Verde Islands.

CHAPTER V

GREAT EXPECTATIONS

July, August, and September in the year 1493 were busy months for Columbus, who had to superintend the buying or building and fitting of ships, the choice and collection of stores, and the selection of his company. There were fourteen caravels, some of them of low tonnage and light draught, and suitable for the navigation of rivers; and three large carracks, or ships of three to four hundred tons. The number of volunteers asked for was a thousand, but at least two thousand applied for permission to go with the expedition, and ultimately some fourteen or fifteen hundred did actually go, one hundred stowaways being included in the number. Unfortunately these adventurers were of a class compared with whom even the cut-throats and gaol-birds of the humble little expedition that had sailed the year before from Palos were useful and efficient. The universal impression about the new lands in the West was that they were places where fortunes could be picked up like dirt, and where the very shores were strewn with gold and precious stones; and every idle scamp in Spain who had a taste for adventure and a desire to get a great deal of money without working for it was anxious to visit the new territory. The result was that instead of artisans, farmers, craftsmen, and colonists, Columbus took with him a company at least half of which consisted of exceedingly well-bred young gentlemen who had no intention of doing any work, but who looked forward to a free and lawless holiday and an early return crowned with wealth and fortune. Although the expedition was primarily for the establishment of a colony, no Spanish women accompanied it; and this was but one of a succession of mistakes and stupidities.

The Admiral, however, was not to be so lonely a person as he had been on his first voyage; friends of his own choice and of a rank that made intimacy possible even with the Captain-General were to accompany him. There was James his brother; there was Friar Bernardo Buil, a Benedictine monk chosen by the Pope to be his apostolic vicar in the New World; there was Alonso de Ojeda, a handsome young aristocrat, cousin to the Inquisitor of Spain, who was distinguished for his dash and strength and pluck; an ideal adventurer, the idol of his fellows, and one of whose daring any number of credible and incredible tales were told. There was Pedro Margarite, a well-born Aragonese, who was destined afterwards to cause much trouble; there was Juan Ponce de Leon, the discoverer of Florida; there was Juan de La Cosa, Columbus's faithful pilot on the Santa Maria on his first voyage; there was Pedro de Las Casas, whose son, at this time a student in Seville, was afterwards to become the historian of the New World and the champion of decency and humanity there. There was also Doctor Chanca, a Court physician who accompanied the expedition not only in his professional capacity but also because his knowledge of botany would enable him to make, a valuable report on the vegetables and fruits of the New World; there was Antonio de Marchena, one of Columbus's oldest friends, who went as astronomer to the expedition. And there was one Coma, who would have remained unknown to this day but that he wrote an exceedingly elegant letter to his friend Nicolo Syllacio in Italy, describing in flowery language the events of the second voyage; which letter, and one written by Doctor Chanca, are the only records of the outward voyage that exist. The journal kept by Columbus on this voyage has been lost, and no copy of it remains.

Columbus settled at Cadiz during the time in which he was engaged upon the fitting out of the expedition. It was no light matter to superintend the appointment of the crews and passengers, every one of whom was probably interviewed by Columbus himself, and at the same time to keep level with Archdeacon Fonseca. This official, it will be remembered, had a disagreement with Columbus as to the number of personal attendants he was to be allowed; and on the matter being referred to the King and Queen they granted Columbus the ridiculous establishment of ten footmen and twenty other servants.

Naturally Fonseca held up his hands and wondered where it would all end. It was no easy matter, moreover, on receipt of letters from the Queen about small matters which occurred to her from time to time, to answer them fully and satisfactorily, and at the same time to make out all the lists of things that would likely be required both for provisioning the voyage and establishing a colony. The provisions carried in those days were not very different from the provisions carried on deep-sea vessels at the present time—except that canned meat, for which, with its horrors and conveniences, the world may hold Columbus responsible, had not then been invented. Unmilled wheat, salted flour, and hard biscuit formed the bulk of the provisions; salted pork was the staple—of the meat supply, with an alternative of salted fish; while cheese, peas, lentils and beans, oil and vinegar, were also carried, and honey and almonds and raisins for the cabin table. Besides water a large provision of rough wine in casks was taken, and the dietary scale would probably compare favourably with that of the British and American mercantile service sixty years ago. In addition a great quantity of seeds of all kinds were taken for planting in Espanola; sugar cane, rice, and vines also, and an equipment of agricultural implements, as well as a selection of horses and other domestic animals for breeding purposes. Twenty mounted soldiers were also carried, and the thousand and one impedimenta of naval, military, and domestic existence.

In the middle of all these preparations news came that a Portuguese caravel had set sail from Madeira in the direction of the new lands. Columbus immediately reported this to the King and Queen, and suggested detaching part of his fleet to pursue her; but instead King John was communicated with, and he declared that if the vessel had sailed as alleged it was without his knowledge and permission, and that he would send three ships after her to recall her—an answer which had to be accepted, although it opened up rather alarming possibilities of four Portuguese vessels reaching the new islands instead of one. Whether these ships ever really sailed or not, or whether the rumour was merely a rumour and an alarm, is not certain; but Columbus was ordered to push on his preparations with the greatest possible speed, to avoid Portuguese waters, but to capture any vessels which he might find in the part of the ocean allotted to Spain, and to inflict summary punishment on the crews. As it turned out he never saw any Portuguese vessels, and before he had returned to Spain again the two nations had come to an amicable agreement quite independently of the Pope and his Bulls. Spain undertook to make no discoveries to the east of the line of demarcation, and Portugal none to the west of it; and so the matter remained until the inhabitants of the discovered lands began to have a voice in their own affairs.

With all his occupations Columbus found time for some amenities, and he had his two sons, Diego and Ferdinand, staying with him at Cadiz. Great days they must have been for these two boys; days filled with excitement and commotion, with the smell of tar and the loading of the innumerable and fascinating materials of life; and many a journey they must have made on the calm waters of Cadiz harbour from ship to ship, dreaming of the distant seas that these high, quaintly carven prows would soon be treading, and the wonderful bays and harbours far away across the world into the waters of which their anchors were to plunge.

September 24th, the day before the fleet sailed, was observed as a festival; and in full ceremonial the blessing of God upon the enterprise was invoked. The ships were hung with flags and with dyed silks and tapestries; every vessel flew the royal standard; and the waters of the harbour resounded with the music of trumpets and harps and pipes and the thunder of artillery. Some Venetian galleys happened to enter the harbour as the fleet was preparing to weigh, and they joined in the salutes and demonstrations which signalled the departure. The Admiral hoisted his flag on the 'Marigalante', one of the largest of the ships; and somewhere among the smaller caravels the little Nina, re-caulked and re-fitted, was also preparing to brave again the dangers over which she had so staunchly prevailed. At sunrise on the 25th the fleet weighed anchor, with all the circumstance and bustle and apparent confusion that accompanies the business of sailing-ships getting under weigh. Up to the last minute

Columbus had his two sons on board with him, and it was not until the ripples were beginning to talk under the bow of the Marigalante that he said good-bye to them and saw them rowed ashore. In bright weather, with a favourable breeze, in glory and dignity, and with high hopes in his heart, the Admiral set out once more on the long sea-road.

CHAPTER VI

THE SECOND VOYAGE

The second voyage of Columbus, profoundly interesting as it must have been to him and to the numerous company to whom these waters were a strange and new region, has not the romantic interest for us that his first voyage had. To the faith that guided him on his first venture knowledge and certainty had now been added; he was going by a familiar road; for to the mariner a road that he has once followed is a road that he knows. As a matter of fact, however, this second voyage was a far greater test of Columbus's skill as a navigator than the first voyage had been. If his navigation had been more haphazard he might never have found again the islands of his first discovery; and the fact that he made a landfall exactly where he wished to make it shows a high degree of exactness in his method of ascertaining latitude, and is another instance of his skill in estimating his dead-reckoning. If he had been equipped with a modern quadrant and Greenwich chronometers he could not have made a quicker voyage nor a more exact landfall.

It will be remembered that he had been obliged to hurry away from Espanola without visiting the islands of the Caribs as he had wished to do. He knew that these islands lay to the south-east of Espanola, and on his second voyage he therefore took a course rather more southerly in order, to make them instead of Guanahani or Espanola. From the day they left Spain his ships had pleasant light airs from the east and north-east which wafted them steadily but slowly on their course. In a week they had reached the Grand Canary, where they paused to make some repairs to one of the ships which, was leaking. Two days later they anchored at Gomera, and loaded up with such supplies as could be procured there better than in Spain. Pigs, goats, sheep and cows were taken on board; domestic fowls also, and a variety of orchard plants and fruit seeds, as well as a provision of oranges, lemons, and melons. They sailed from Gomera on the 7th of October, but the winds were so light that it was a week later before they had passed Ferro and were once more in the open Atlantic.

On setting his course from Ferro Columbus issued sealed instructions to the captain of each ship which, in the event of the fleet becoming scattered, would guide them to the harbour of La Navidad in Espanola; but the captains had strict orders not to open these instructions unless their ships became separated from the fleet, as Columbus still wished to hold for himself the secret of this mysterious road to the west. There were no disasters, however, and no separations. The trade wind blew soft and steady, wafting them south and west; and because of the more southerly course steered on this voyage they did not even encounter the weed of the Sargasso Sea, which they left many leagues on their starboard hand. The only incident of the voyage was a sudden severe hurricane, a brief summer tempest which raged throughout one night and terrified a good many of the voyagers, whose superstitious fears were only allayed when they saw the lambent flames of the light of Saint Elmo playing about the rigging of the Admiral's ship. It was just the Admiral's luck that this phenomenon should be observed over his ship and over none of the others; it added to his prestige as a person peculiarly favoured by the divine protection, and confirmed his own belief that he held a heavenly as well as a royal commission.

The water supply had been calculated a little too closely, and began to run low. The hurried preparation of the ships had resulted as usual in bad work; most of them were leaking, and the crew were constantly at work at the pumps; and there was the usual discontent. Columbus, however, knew by the signs as well as by his dead-reckoning that he was somewhere close to land; and with a fine demonstration of confidence he increased the ration of water, instead of lowering it, assuring the crews that they would be ashore in a day or two. On Saturday evening, November 2nd, although no land was in sight, Columbus was so sure of his position that he ordered the fleet to take in sail and go on slowly until morning. As the Sunday dawned and the sky to the west was cleared of the morning bank of clouds the look-out on the Marigalante reported land ahead; and sure enough the first sunlight of that day showed them a green and verdant island a few leagues away.

As they approached it Columbus christened it Dominica in honour of the day on which it was discovered. He sailed round it; but as there was no harbour, and as another island was in sight to the north, he sailed on in that direction. This little island he christened Marigalante; and going ashore with his retinue he hoisted the royal banner, and formally took possession of the whole group of six islands which were visible from the high ground. There were no inhabitants on the island, but the voyagers spent some hours wandering about its tangled woods and smelling the rich odours of spice, and tasting new and unfamiliar fruits. They next sailed on to an island to the north which Columbus christened Guadaloupe as a memorial of the shrine in Estremadura to which he had made a pious pilgrimage. They landed on this island and remained a week there, in the course of which they made some very remarkable discoveries.

The villagers were not altogether unfriendly, although they were shy at first; but red caps and hawks' bells had their usual effect. There were signs of warfare, in the shape of bone-tipped arrows; there were tame parrots much larger than those of the northern islands; they found pottery and rough wood carving, and the unmistakable stern timber of a European vessel. But they discovered stranger things than that. They found human skulls used as household utensils, and gruesome fragments of human bodies, unmistakable remains of a feast; and they realised that at last they were in the presence of a man-eating tribe. Later they came to know, something of the habits of the islanders; how they made raiding expeditions to the neighbouring islands, and carried off large numbers of prisoners, retaining the women as concubines and eating the men. The boys were mutilated and fattened like capons, being employed as labourers until they had arrived at years of discretion, at which point they were killed and eaten, as these cannibal epicures did not care for the flesh of women and boys. There were a great number of women on the island, and many of them were taken off to the ships—with their own consent, according to Doctor Chanca. The men, however, eluded the Spaniards and would not come on board, having doubtless very clear views about the ultimate destination of men who were taken prisoners. Some women from a neighbouring island, who had been captured by the cannibals, came to Columbus and begged to be taken on board his ship for protection; but instead of receiving them he decked them with ornaments and sent them ashore again. The cannibals artfully stripped off their ornaments and sent them back to get some more.

The peculiar habits of the islanders added an unusual excitement to shore leave, and there was as a rule no trouble in collecting the crews and bringing them off to the ships at nightfall. But on one evening it was discovered that one of the captains and eight men had not returned. An exploring party was sent of to search for them, but they came back without having found anything, except a village in the middle of the forest from which the inhabitants had fled at their approach, leaving behind them in the cooking pots a half-cooked meal of human remains—an incident which gave the explorers a distaste for further search. Young Alonso de Ojeda, however, had no fear of the cannibals; this was just the kind of occasion in which he revelled; and he offered to take a party of forty men into the interior to search for the missing men. He went right across the island, but was able to discover nothing except birds and fruits and unknown trees; and Columbus, in great distress of mind, had to give up his men for lost. He took in wood and water, and was on the point of weighing anchor when the missing men appeared on the shore and signalled for a boat. It appeared that they had got lost in a tangled forest in the interior, that they had tried to climb the trees in order to get their bearings by the stars, but without success; and that they had finally struck the sea-shore and followed it until they had arrived opposite the anchorage.

They brought some women and boys with them, and the fleet must now have had a large number of these willing or unwilling captives. This was the first organised transaction of slavery on the part of Columbus, whose design was to send slaves regularly back to Spain in exchange for the cattle and supplies necessary for the colonies. There was not very much said now about religious conversion, but only about exchanging the natives for cattle. The fine point of Christopher's philosophy on this subject had been rubbed off; he had taken the first step a year ago on the beach at Guanahani, and after that the road opened out broad before him. Slaves for cattle, and cattle for the islands; and wealth from cattle and islands for Spain, and payment from Spain for Columbus, and money from Columbus for the redemption of the Holy Sepulchre—these were the links in the chain of hope that bound him to his pious idea. He had seen the same thing done by the Portuguese on the Guinea coast, and it never occurred to him that there was anything the matter with it. On the contrary, at this time his idea was only to take slaves from among the Caribs and man-eating islanders as a punishment for their misdeeds; but this, like his other fine ideas, soon had to give way before the tide of greed and conquest.

The Admiral was now anxious to get back to La Navidad, and discover the condition of the colony which he had left behind him there. He therefore sailed from Guadaloupe on November 20th and steered to the north-west. His captive islanders told him that the mainland lay to the south; and if he had listened to them and sailed south he would have probably landed on the coast of South America in a fortnight. He shaped his course instead to the north-west, passing many islands, but not pausing until the 14th, when he reached the island named by him Santa Cruz. He found more Caribs here, and his men had a brush with them, one of the crew being wounded by a poisoned arrow of which he died in a few days. The Carib Chiefs were captured and put in irons. They sailed again and passed a group of islets which Columbus named after Saint Ursula and the Eleven Thousand Virgins; discovered Porto Rico also, in one of the beautiful harbours of which they anchored and stayed for two days. Sailing now to the west they made land again on the 22nd of November; and coasting along it they soon sighted the mountain of Monte Christi, and Columbus recognised that he was on the north coast of Espanola.

CHAPTER VII

THE EARTHLY PARADISE REVISITED

On the 25th November 1493, Columbus once more dropped his anchor in the harbour of Monte Christi, and a party was sent ashore to prospect for a site suitable for the new town which he intended to build, for he was not satisfied with the situation of La Navidad. There was a large river close by; and while the party was surveying the land they came suddenly upon two dead bodies lying by the river-side, one with a rope round its neck and the other with a rope round its feet. The bodies were too much decomposed to be recognisable; nevertheless to the party rambling about in the sunshine and stillness of that green place the discovery was a very gruesome one. They may have thought much, but they said little. They returned to the ship, and resumed their search on the next day, when they found two more corpses, one of which was seen to have a large quantity of beard. As all the natives were beardless this was a very significant and unpleasant discovery, and the explorers returned at once and reported what they had seen to Columbus. He thereupon set sail for La Navidad, but the navigation off that part of the coast was necessarily slow because of the number of the shoals and banks, on one of which the Admiral's ship had been lost the year before; and the short voyage occupied three days.

They arrived at La Navidad late on the evening of the 27th—too late to make it advisable to land. Some natives came out in a canoe, rowed round the Admiral's ship, stopped and looked at it, and then rowed away again. When the fleet had anchored Columbus ordered two guns to be fired; but there was no response except from the echoes that went rattling among the islands, and from the frightened birds that rose screaming and circling from the shore. No guns and no signal fires; no sign of human habitation whatever; and no sound out of the weird darkness except the lap of the water and the call of the birds . . . . The night passed in anxiety and depression, and in a certain degree of nervous tension, which was relieved at two or three o'clock in the morning by the sound of paddles and the looming of a canoe through the dusky starlight. Native voices were heard from the canoe asking in a loud voice for the Admiral; and when the visitors had been directed to the Marigalante they refused to go on board until Columbus himself had spoken to them, and they had seen by the light of a lantern that it was the Admiral himself. The chief of them was a cousin of Guacanagari, who said that the King was ill of a wound in his leg, or that he would certainly have come himself to welcome the Admiral. The Spaniards? Yes, they were well, said the young chief; or rather, he added ominously, those that remained were well, but some had died of illness, and some had been killed in quarrels that had arisen among them. He added that the province had been invaded by two neighbouring kings who had burned many of the native houses. This news, although grave, was a relief from the dreadful uncertainty that had prevailed in the early part of the night, and the Admiral's company, somewhat consoled, took a little sleep.

In the morning a party was sent ashore to La Navidad. Not a boat was in sight, nor any native canoes; the harbour was silent and deserted. When the party had landed and gone up to the place where the fort had been built they found no fort there; only the blackened and charred remains of a fort. The whole thing had been burned level with the ground, and amid the blackened ruins they found pieces of rag and clothing. The natives, instead of coming to greet them, lurked guiltily behind trees, and when they were seen fled away into the woods. All this was very disquieting indeed, and in significant contrast to their behaviour of the year before. The party from the ship threw buttons and beads and bells to the retiring natives in order to try and induce them to come forward, but only four approached, one of whom was a relation of Guacanagari. These four consented to go into the boat and to be rowed out to the ship. Columbus then spoke to them through his interpreter; and they admitted what had been only too obvious to the party that went ashore—that the Spaniards were all dead, and that not one of the garrison remained. It seemed that two neighbouring kings, Caonabo and Mayreni, had made an attack upon the fort, burned the buildings, and killed and wounded most of the defenders; and that Guacanagari, who had been fighting on their behalf, had also been wounded and been obliged to retire. The natives offered to go and fetch Guacanagari himself, and departed with that object.

In the greatest anxiety the Admiral and his company passed that day and night waiting for the King to come. Early the next morning Columbus himself went ashore and visited the spot where the settlement had been. There he found destruction whole and complete, with nothing but a few rags of clothing as an evidence that the place had ever been inhabited by human beings. As Guacanagari did not appear some of the Spaniards began to suspect that he had had a hand in the matter, and proposed immediate reprisal; but Columbus, believing still in the man who had "loved him so much that it was wonderful" did not take this view, and his belief in Guacanagari's loyalty was confirmed by the discovery that his own dwelling had also been burned down.

Columbus set some of his party searching in the ditch of the fort in case any treasure should have been buried there, as he had ordered it should be in event of danger, and while this was going on he walked along the coast for a few miles to visit a spot which he thought might be suitable for the new settlement. At a distance of a mile or two he found a village of seven or eight huts from which the inhabitants fled at his approach, carrying such of their goods as were portable, and leaving the rest hidden in the grass. Here were found several things that had belonged to the Spaniards and which were not likely to have been bartered; new Moorish mantles, stockings, bolts of cloth, and one of the Admiral's lost anchors; other articles also, among them a dead man's head wrapped up with great care in a small basket. Shaking their own living heads, Columbus and his party returned. Suddenly they came on some suspicious-looking mounds of earth over which new grass was growing. An examination of these showed them to be the graves of eleven of the Spaniards, the remains of the clothing being quite sufficient to identify them. Doctor Chanca, who examined them, thought that they had not been dead two months. Speculation came to an end in the face of this eloquent certainty; there were the dead bodies of some of the colonists; and the voyagers knelt round with bare heads while the bodies were replaced in the grave and the ceremony of Christian burial performed over them.

Little by little the dismal story was elicited from the natives, who became less timid when they saw that the Spaniards meant them no harm. It seemed that Columbus had no sooner gone away than the colonists began to abandon themselves to every kind of excess. While the echo of the Admiral's wise counsels was yet in their ears they began to disobey his orders. Honest work they had no intention of doing, and although Diego Arana, their commander, did his best to keep order, and although one or two of the others were faithful to him and to Columbus, their authority was utterly insufficient to check the lawless folly of the rest. Instead of searching for gold mines, they possessed themselves by force of every ounce of gold they could steal or seize from the natives, treating them with both cruelty and contempt. More brutal excesses followed as a matter of course. Guacanagari, in his kindly indulgence and generosity, had allowed them to take three native wives apiece, although he himself and his people were content with one. But of course the Spaniards had thrown off all restraint, however mild, and ran amok among the native inhabitants, seizing their wives and seducing their daughters. Upon this naturally followed dissensions among themselves, jealousy coming hot upon the heels of unlawful possession; and, in the words of Irving, "the natives beheld with astonishment the beings whom they had worshipped as descended from the skies abandoned to the grossest of earthly passions and raging against each other with worse than brutal ferocity."

Upon their strifes and dissensions followed another breach of the Admiral's wise regulations; they no longer cared to remain together in the fort, but split up into groups and went off with their women into the woods, reverting to a savagery beside which the gentle existence of the natives was high civilisation. There were squabbles and fights in which one or two of the Spaniards were killed; and Pedro Gutierrez and Rodrigo de Escovedo, whom Columbus had appointed as lieutenants to Arana, headed a faction of revolt against his authority, and took themselves off with nine other Spaniards and a great number of women. They had heard a great deal about the mines of Cibao, and they decided to go in search of them and secure their treasures for themselves. They went inland into a territory which was under the rule of King Caonabo, a very fierce Carib who was not a native of Espanola, but had come there as an adventurer and remained as a conqueror. Although he resented the intrusion of the Spaniards into the island he would not have dared to come and attack them there if they had obeyed the Admiral's orders and remained in the territory of Guacanagari; but when they came into his own country he had them in a trap, and it was easy for him to fall upon those foolish swaggering Spaniards and put them to death. He then decided to go and take the fort.

He formed an alliance with the neighbouring king, Mayreni, whose province was in the west of the island. Getting together a force of warriors these two kings marched rapidly and stealthily through the, forest for several days until they arrived at its northern border. They came in the dead of night to the neighbourhood of La Navidad, where the inhabitants of the fortress, some ten in number, were fast asleep. Fast asleep were the remaining dozen or so of the Spaniards who were living in houses or huts in the neighbourhood; fast asleep also the gentle natives, not dreaming of troubles from any quarter but that close at hand. The sweet silence of the tropical night was suddenly broken by frightful yells as Caonabo and his warriors rushed the fortress and butchered the inhabitants, setting fire to it and to the houses round about. As their flimsy huts burst into flames the surprised Spaniards rushed out, only to be fallen upon by the infuriated blacks. Eight of the Spaniards rushed naked into the sea and were drowned; the rest were butchered. Guacanagari manfully came to their assistance and with his own followers fought throughout the night; but his were a gentle and unwarlike people, and they were easily routed. The King himself was badly wounded in the thigh, but Caonabo's principal object seems to have been the destruction of the Spaniards, and when that was completed he and his warriors, laden with the spoils, retired.

Thus Columbus, walking on the shore with his native interpreter, or sitting in his cabin listening with knitted brow to the accounts of the islanders, learns of the complete and utter failure of his first hopes. It has come to this. These are the real first-fruits of his glorious conquest and discovery. The New World has served but as a virgin field for the Old Adam. He who had sought to bring light and life to these happy islanders had brought darkness and death; they had innocently clasped the sword he had extended to them and cut themselves. The Christian occupation of the New World had opened with vice, cruelty, and destruction; the veil of innocence had been rent in twain, and could never be mended or joined again. And the Earthly Paradise in which life had gone so happily, of which sun and shower had been the true rulers, and the green sprouting harvests the only riches, had been turned into a shambles by the introduction of human rule and civilised standards of wealth. Gold first and then women, things beautiful and innocent in the happy native condition of the islands, had been the means of the disintegration and death of this first colony. These are serious considerations for any coloniser; solemn considerations for a discoverer who is only on the verge and beginning of his empire-making; mournful considerations for Christopher as he surveys the blackened ruins of the fort, or stands bare-headed by the grass-covered graves.

There seemed to be a certain hesitancy on the part of Guacanagari to present himself; for though he kept announcing his intention of coming to visit the Admiral he did not come. A couple of days after the discovery of the remains, however, he sent a message to Columbus begging him to come and see him, which the Admiral accordingly did, accompanied by a formal retinue and carrying with him the usual presents. Guacanagari was in bed sure enough complaining of a wounded leg, and he told the story of the settlement very much as Columbus had already heard it from the other natives. He pointed to his own wounded leg as a sign that he had been loyal and faithful to his friendly promises; but when the leg was examined by the surgeon in order that it might be dressed no wound could be discovered, and it was obvious to Doctor Chanca that the skin had not been broken. This seemed odd; Friar Buil was so convinced that the whole story was a deception that he wished the Admiral to execute Guacanagari on the spot. Columbus, although he was puzzled, was by no means convinced that Guacanagari had been unfaithful to him, and decided to do nothing for the present. He invited the cacique to come on board the flagship; which he did, being greatly interested by some of the Carib prisoners, notably a handsome woman, named by the Spaniards Doña Catalina, with whom he held a long conversation.

Relations between the Admiral and the cacique, although outwardly cordial, were altogether different from what they had been in, the happy days after their first meeting; the man seemed to shrink from all the evidence of Spanish power, and when they proposed to hang a cross round his neck the native king, much as he loved trinkets and toys, expressed a horror and fear of this jewel when he learned that it was an emblem of the Christian faith. He had seen a little too much of the Christian religion; and Heaven only knows with what terror and depression the emblem of the cross inspired him. He went ashore; and when a messenger was sent to search for

28

him a few days afterwards, it was found that he had moved his whole establishment into the interior of the island. The beautiful native woman Catalina escaped to shore and disappeared at the same time; and the two events were connected in the minds of some of the Spaniards, and held, wrongly as it turned out, to be significant of a deep plot of native treachery.

The most urgent need was to build the new settlement and lay out a town. Several small parties were sent out to reconnoitre the coast in both directions, but none of them found a suitable place; and on December 7th the whole fleet sailed to the east in the hope of finding a better position. They were driven by adverse winds into a harbour some thirty miles to the east of Monte Christi, and when they went ashore they decided that this was as good a site as any for the new town. There was about a quarter of a mile of level sandy beach enclosed by headlands on either side; there was any amount of rock and stones for building, and there was a natural barrier of hills and mountains a mile or so inland that would protect a camp from that side.—The soil was very fertile, the vegetation luxuriant; and the mango swamps a little way inland drained into a basin or lake which provided an unlimited water supply. Columbus therefore set about establishing a little town, to which he gave the name of Isabella. Streets and squares were laid out, and rows of temporary buildings made of wood and thatched with grass were hastily run up for the accommodation of the members of the expedition, while the foundations of three stone buildings were also marked out and the excavations put in hand. These buildings were the church, the storehouse, and a residence for Columbus as Governor-General. The stores were landed, the horses and cattle accommodated ashore, the provisions, ammunition, and agricultural implements also. Labourers were set to digging out the foundations of the stone buildings, carpenters to cutting down trees and running up the light wooden houses that were to serve as barracks for the present; masons were employed in hewing stones and building landing-piers; and all the crowd of well-born adventurers were set to work with their hands, much to their disgust. This was by no means the life they had imagined, and at the first sign of hard work they turned sulky and discontented. There was, to be sure, some reason for their discontent. Things had not quite turned out as Columbus had promised they should; there was no store of gold, nor any sign of great desire on the part of the natives to bring any; and to add to their other troubles, illness began to break out in the camp. The freshly-turned rank soil had a bad effect on the health of the garrison; the lake, which had promised to be so pleasant a feature in the new town, gave off dangerous malarial vapours at night; and among the sufferers from this trouble was Columbus himself, who endured for some weeks all the pains and lassitude of the disagreeable fever.

The ships were now empty and ready for the return voyage, and as soon as Columbus was better he set to work to face the situation. After all his promises it would never do to send them home empty or in ballast; a cargo of stones from the new-found Indies would not be well received in Spain. The natives had told him that somewhere in the island existed the gold mines of Cibao, and he determined to make an attempt to find these, so that he could send his ships home laden with a cargo that would be some indemnity for the heavy cost of the expedition and some compensation for the bad news he must write with regard to his first settlement. Young Ojeda was chosen to lead an expedition of fifteen picked men into the interior; and as the gold mines were said to be in a part of the island not under the command of Guacanagari, but in the territory of the dreaded Caonabo, there was no little anxiety felt about the expedition.

Ojeda started in the beginning of January 1494, and marched southwards through dense forests until, having crossed a mountain range, he came down into a beautiful and fertile valley, where they were hospitably received by the natives. They saw plenty of gold in the sand of the river that watered the valley, which sand the natives had a way of washing so that the gold was separated from it; and there seemed to be so much wealth there that Ojeda hurried back to the new city of Isabella to make his report to Columbus. The effect upon the discontented colonists was remarkable. Once more everything was right; wealth beyond the dreams of avarice was at their hand; and all they had to do was to stretch out their arms and take it. Columbus felt that he need no longer delay the despatch of twelve of his ships on the homeward voyage. If he had not got golden cargoes for them, at any rate he had got the next best thing, which was the certainty of gold; and it did not matter whether it was in the ships or in his storehouse. He had news to send home at any rate, and a great variety of things to ask for in return, and he therefore set about writing his report to the Sovereigns. Other people, as we know, were writing letters too; the reiterated promise of gold, and the marvellous anecdotes which these credulous settlers readily believed from the natives, such as that there was a rock close by out of which gold would burst if you struck it with a club, raised greed and expectation in Spain to a fever pitch, and prepared the reaction which followed.

We may now read the account of the New World as Columbus sent it home to the King and Queen of Spain in the end of January 1494, and as they read it some weeks later. Their comments, written in the margin of the original, are printed in italics at the end of each paragraph. It was drawn up in the form of a memorandum, and entrusted to Antonio de Torres, who was commanding the return expedition.

"What you, Antonio de Torres, captain of the ship Marigalante and Alcalde of the City of Isabella, are to say and supplicate on my part to the King and Queen, our Lords, is as follows:—

"First. Having delivered the letters of credence which you carry from me for their Highnesses, you will kiss for me their Royal feet and hands and will recommend me to their Highnesses as to a King and Queen, my natural Lords, in whose service I desire to end my days: as you will be able to say this more fully to their Highnesses, according to what you have seen and known of me.

["Their Highnesses hold him in their favour.]

"Item. Although by the letters I write to their Highnesses, and also the father Friar Buil and the Treasurer, they will be able to understand all that has been done here since our arrival, and this very minutely and extensively: nevertheless, you will say to their Highnesses on my part, that it has pleased God to give me such favour in their service, that up to the present time. I do not find less, nor has less been found in anything than what I wrote and said and affirmed to their Highnesses in the past: but rather, by the Grace of God, I hope that it will appear, by works much more clearly and very soon, because such signs and indications of spices have been found on the shores of the sea alone, without having gone inland, that there is reason that very much better results may be hoped for: and this also may be hoped for in the mines of gold, because by two persons only who went to investigate, each one on his own part, without remaining there because there was not many people, so many rivers have been discovered so filled with gold, that all who saw it and gathered specimens of it with the hands alone, came away so pleased and say such things in regard to its abundance, that I am timid about telling it and writing it to their Highnesses: but because Gorbalan, who was one of the discoverers, is going yonder, he will tell what he saw, although another named Hojeda remains here, a servant of the Duke of Medinaceli, a very discreet youth and very prudent, who without doubt and without comparison even, discovered much more according to the memorandum which he brought of the rivers, saying that there is an incredible quantity in each one of them for this their Highnesses may give thanks to God, since He has been so favourable to them in all their affairs.

["Their Highnesses give many thanks to God for this, and consider as a very signal service all that the Admiral has done in this matter and is doing: because they know that after God they are indebted to him for all they have had, and will have in this affair: and as they are writing him more fully about this, they refer him to their letter.]

31

"Item. You will say to their Highnesses, although I already have written it to them, that I desired greatly to be able to send them a larger quantity of gold in this fleet, from that which it is hoped may be gathered here, but the greater part of our people who are here, have fallen suddenly ill: besides, this fleet cannot remain here longer, both on account of the great expense it occasions and because this time is suitable for those persons who are to bring the things which are greatly needed here, to go and be able to return: as, if they delay going away from here, those who are to return will not be able to do so by May: and besides this, if I wished to undertake to go to the mines or rivers now, with the well people who are here, both on the sea and in the settlement on land, I would have many difficulties and even dangers, because in order to go twenty-three or twenty-four leagues from here where there are harbours and rivers to cross, and in order to cover such a long route and reach there at the time which would be necessary to gather the gold, a large quantity of provisions would have to be carried, which cannot be carried on the shoulders, nor are there beasts of burden here which could be used for this purpose: nor are the roads and passes sufficiently prepared, although I have commenced to get them in readiness so as to be passable: and also it was very inconvenient to leave the sick here in an open place, in huts, with the provisions and supplies which are on land: for although these Indians may have shown themselves to the discoverers and show themselves every day, to be very simple and not malicious nevertheless, as they come here among us each day, it did not appear that it would be a good idea to risk losing these people and the supplies. This loss an Indian with a piece of burning wood would be able to cause by setting fire to the huts, because they are always going and coming by night and by day: on their account, we have guards in the camp, while the settlement is open and defenceless.

["That he did well.]

"Moreover, as we have seen among those who went by land to make discoveries that the greater part fell sick after returning, and some of them even were obliged to turn back on the road, it was also reasonable to fear that the same thing would happen to those who are well, who would now go, and as a consequence they would run the risk of two dangers: the one, that of falling sick yonder, in the same work, where there is no house nor any defence against that cacique who is called Caonabb, who is a very bad man according to all accounts, and much more audacious and who, seeing us there, sick and in such disorder, would be able to undertake what he would not dare if we were well: and with this difficulty there is another—that of bringing here what gold we might obtain, because we must either bring a small quantity and go and come each day and undergo the risk of sickness, or it must be sent with some part of the people, incurring the same danger of losing it.

["He did well.]

"So that, you will say to their Highnesses, that these are the causes why the fleet has not been at present detained, and why more gold than the specimens has not been sent them: but confiding in the mercy of God, who in everything and for everything has guided us as far as here, these people will quickly become convalescent, as they are already doing, because only certain places in the country suit them and they then recover; and it is certain that if they had some fresh meat in order to convalesce, all with the aid of God would very quickly be on foot, and even the greater part would already be convalescent at this time: nevertheless they will be re-established. With the few healthy ones who remain here, each day work is done toward enclosing the settlement and placing it in a state of some defence and the supplies in safety, which will be accomplished in a short time, because it is to be only a small dry wall. For the Indians are not a people to undertake anything unless they should find us sleeping, even though they might have thought of it in the manner in which they served the others who remained here. Only on account of their (the Spaniards') lack of caution—they being so few—and the great opportunities they gave the Indians to have and do what they did, they would never have dared to undertake to injure them if they had seen that they were cautious. And this work being finished, I will then undertake to go to the said rivers, either starting upon the road from here and seeking the best possible expedients, or going around the island by sea as far as that place from which it is said it cannot be more than six or seven leagues to the said rivers. In such a manner that the gold can be gathered and placed in security in some fortress or tower which can then be constructed there, in order to keep it securely until the time when the two caravels return here, and in order that then, with the first suitable weather for sailing this course, it may be sent to a place of safety.

["That this is well and must be done in this manner.]

"Item. You will say to their Highnesses, as has been said, that the cause of the general sicknesses common to all is the change of water and air, because we see that it extends to all conditions and few are in danger: consequently, for the preservation of health, after God, it is necessary that these people be provided with the provisions to which they are accustomed in Spain, because neither they, nor others who may come anew, will be able to serve their Highnesses if they are not well: and this provision must continue until a supply is accumulated here from what shall be sowed and planted here. I say wheat and barley, and vines, of which little has been done this year because a site for the town could not be selected before, and then when it was selected the few labourers who were here became sick, and they, even though they had been well, had so few and such lean and meagre beasts of burden, that they were able to do but little: nevertheless, they have sown something, more in order to try the soil which appears very wonderful, so that from it some relief may be hoped in our necessities. We are very sure, as the result makes it apparent to us, that in this country wheat as well as the vine will grow very well: but the fruit must be waited for, which, if it corresponds to the quickness with which the wheat grows and of some few vine-shoots which were planted, certainly will not cause regret here for the productions of Andalusia or Sicily: neither is it different with the sugar-canes according to the manner in which some few that were planted have grown. For it is certain that the sight of the land of these islands, as well of the mountains and sierras and waters as of the plains where there are rich rivers, is so beautiful, that no other land on which the sun shines can appear better or as beautiful.

["Since the land is such, it must be managed that the greatest possible quantity of all things shall be sown, and Don Juan de Fonseca is to be written to send continually all that is necessary for this purpose.]

"Item. You will say that, inasmuch as much of the wine which the fleet brought was wasted on this journey, and this, according to what the greater number say, was because of the bad workmanship which the coopers did in Seville, the greatest necessity we feel here at the present time is for wines, and it is what we desire most to have and although we may have biscuit as well as wheat sufficient for a longer time, nevertheless it is necessary that a reasonable quantity should also be sent, because the journey is long and provision cannot be made each day and in the same manner some salted meat, I say bacon, and other salt meat better than that we brought on this journey. It is necessary that each time a caravel comes here, fresh meat shall be sent, and even more than that, lambs and little ewe lambs, more females than males, and some little yearling calves, male and female, and some he-asses and she-asses and some mares for labour and breeding, as there are none of these animals here of any value or which can be made use of by man. And because I apprehend that their Highnesses may not be, in Seville, and that the officials or ministers will not provide these things without their express order, and as it is necessary they should come at the first opportunity, and as in consultation and reply the time for the departure of the vessels-which must be here during all of May-will be past: you will say to their Highnesses that I charged and commanded you to pledge the gold you are carrying yonder and place it in possession of some merchant in Seville, who will furnish therefor the necessary maravedis to load two caravels with wine and wheat and the other things of which you are taking a memorandum; which merchant will carry or send the said gold to their Highnesses that they may see it and receive it, and cause what shall have been expended for fitting out and loading of the said two caravels to be paid: and in order to comfort and strengthen these people remaining here, the utmost efforts must be made for the return of these caravels for all the month of May, that the people before commencing the summer may see and have some refreshment from these things, especially the invalids: the things of which we are already in great need here are such as raisins, sugar, almonds, honey and rice, which should have been sent in large quantities and very little was sent, and that which came is already used and consumed, and even the greater part of the medicines which were brought from there, on account of the multitude of sick people. You are carrying memoranda signed by my hand, as has been said, of things for the people in good health as well as for the sick. You will provide these things fully if the money is sufficient, or at least the things which it is most necessary to send at once, in order that the said two vessels can bring them, and you can arrange with their Highnesses, to have the remaining things sent by other vessels as quickly as possible.

["Their Highnesses sent an order to Don Juan de Fonseca to obtain at once information about the persons who committed the fraud of the casks, and to cause all the damage to the wine to be recovered from them, with the costs: and he must see that the canes which are sent are of good quality, and that the other things mentioned here are provided at once.]

"Item. You will say to their Highnesses that as there is no language here by means of which these people can be made to understand our Holy Faith, as your Highnesses and also we who are here desire, although we will do all we can towards it—I am sending some of the cannibals in the vessels, men and women and male and female children, whom their Highnesses can order placed with persons from whom they can better learn the language, making use of them in service, and ordering that little by little more pains be taken with them than with other slaves, that they may learn one from the other: if they do not see or speak with each other until some time has passed, they will learn more quickly there than here, and will be better interpreters—although we will not cease to do as much as possible here. It is true that as there is little intercourse between these people from one island to another, there is some difference in their language, according to how far distant they are from each other. And as, of the other islands, those of the cannibals are very large and very well populated, it would appear best to take some of their men and women and send them yonder to Castile, because by taking them away, it may cause them to abandon at once that inhuman custom which they have of eating men: and by learning the language there in Castile, they will receive baptism much more quickly, and provide for the safety of their souls. Even among the peoples who are not cannibals we shall gain great credit, by their seeing that we can seize and take captive those from whom they are accustomed to receive injuries, and of whom they are in such terror that they are frightened by one man alone. You will certify to their Highnesses that the arrival here and sight of such a fine fleet all together has inspired very great authority here and assured very great security for future things: because all the people on this great island and in the other islands, seeing the good treatment which those who well behave receive, and the bad treatment given to those who behave ill, will very quickly render obedience, so that they can be considered as vassals of their Highnesses. And as now they not only do willingly whatever is required of them by our people, but further, they voluntarily undertake everything which they understand may please us, their Highnesses may also be certain that in many respects, as much for the present as for the future, the coming of this fleet has given them a great reputation, and not less yonder among the Christian princes: which their Highnesses will be better able to consider and understand than I can tell them.

["That he is to be told what has befallen the cannibals who came here. That it is very well and must be done in this manner, but that he must try there as much as possible to bring them to our Holy Catholic faith and do the same with the inhabitants of the islands where he is.]

"Item. You will say to their Highnesses that the safety of the souls of the said cannibals, and further of those here, has inspired the thought that the more there are taken yonder, the better it will be, and their Highnesses can be served by it in this manner: having seen how necessary the flocks and beasts of burden are here, for the sustenance of the people who must be here, and even of all these islands, their Highnesses can give licence and permission to a sufficient number of caravels to come here each year, and bring the said flocks and other supplies and things to settle the country and make use of the land: and this at reasonable prices at the expense of those who bring them: and these things can be paid for in slaves from among these cannibals, a very proud and comely people, well proportioned and of good intelligence, who having been freed from that inhumanity, we believe will be better than any other slaves. They will be freed from this cruelty as soon as they are outside their country, and many of them can be taken with the row-boats which it is known how to build here: it being understood, however, that a trustworthy person shall be placed on each one of the caravels coming here, who shall forbid the said caravels to stop at any other place or island than this place, where the loading and unloading of all the merchandise must be done. And further, their Highnesses will be able to establish their rights over these slaves which are taken from here yonder to Spain. And you will bring or send a reply to this, in order that the necessary preparations may be made here with more confidence if it appears well to their Highnesses.

["This project must be held in abeyance for the present until another method is suggested from there, and the Admiral may write what he thinks in regard to it.]

"Item. Also you will say to their Highnesses that it is more profitable and costs less to hire the vessels as the merchants hire them for Flanders, by tons, rather than in any other manner: therefore I charged you to hire the two caravels which you are to send here, in this manner: and all the others which their Highnesses send here can be hired thus, if they consider it for their service but I do not intend to say this of those vessels which are to come here with their licence, for the slave trade.

["Their Highnesses order Don Juan de Fonseca to hire the caravels in this manner if it can be done.]

"Item. You will say to their Highnesses, that to avoid any further cost, I bought these caravels of which you are taking a memorandum in order to retain them here with these two ships: that is to say the Gallega and that other, the Capitana, of which I likewise purchased the three-eighths from the master of it, for the price given in the said memorandum which you are taking, signed by my hand. These ships not only will give authority and great security to the people who are obliged to remain inland and make arrangements with the Indians to gather the gold, but they will also be of service in any other dangerous matter which may arise with a strange people; besides the caravels are necessary for the discovery of the mainland and the other islands which lie between here and there: and you will entreat their Highnesses to order the maravedis which these ships cost, paid at the times which they have been promised, because without doubt they will soon receive what they cost, according to what I believe and hope in the mercy of God.

["The Admiral has done well, and to tell him that the sum has been paid here to the one who sold the ship, and Don Juan de Fonseca has been ordered to pay for the two caravels which the Admiral bought.]

"Item. You will say to their Highnesses, and will supplicate on my part as humbly as possible, that it may please them to reflect on what they will learn most fully from the letters and other writings in regard to the peace and tranquillity and concord of those who are here: and that for the service of their Highnesses such persons may be selected as shall not be suspected, and who will give more attention to the matters for which they are sent than to their own interests: and since you saw and knew everything in regard to this matter, you will speak and will tell their Highnesses the truth about all the things as you understood them, and you will endeavour that the provision which their Highnesses make in regard to it shall come with the first ships if possible, in order that there may be no scandals here in a matter of so much importance in the service of their Highnesses.

["Their Highnesses are well informed in regard to this matter, and suitable provision will be made for everything.]

"Item. You will tell their Highnesses of the situation of this city, and the beauty of the surrounding province as you saw and understood it, and how I made you its Alcade, by the powers which I have for same from their Highnesses: whom I humbly entreat to hold the said provision in part satisfaction of your services, as I hope from their Highnesses.

["It pleases their Highnesses that you shall be Alcade.]

"Item. Because Mosen Pedro Margarite, servant of their Highnesses, has done good service, and I hope he will do the same henceforward in matters which are entrusted to him, I have been pleased to have him remain here, and also Gaspar and Beltran, because they are recognised servants of their Highnesses, in order to intrust them with matters of confidence. You will specialty entreat their Highnesses in regard to the said Mosen Pedro, who is married and has children, to provide him with some charge in the order of Santiago, whose habit he wears, that his wife and children may have the wherewith to live. In the same manner you will relate how well and diligently Juan Aguado, servant of their Highnesses, has rendered service in everything which he has been ordered to do, and that I supplicate their Highnesses to have him and the aforesaid persons in their charge and to reward them.

["Their Highnesses order 30,000 maravedis to be assigned to Mosen Pedro each year, and to Gaspar and Beltran, to each one, 15,000 maravedis each year, from the present, August 15, 1494, henceforward: and thus the Admiral shall cause to be paid to them whatever must be paid yonder in the Indies, and Don Juan de Fonseca whatever must be paid here: and in regard to Juan Iguado, their Highnesses will hold him in remembrance.]

"Item. You will tell their Highnesses of the labour performed by Dr. Chanca, confronted with so many invalids, and still more because of the lack of provisions and nevertheless, he acts with great diligence and charity in everything pertaining to his office. And as their Highnesses referred to me the salary which he was to receive here, because, being here, it is certain that he cannot take or receive anything from any one, nor earn money by his office as he earned it in Castile, or would be able to earn it being at his ease and living in a different manner from the way he lives here; therefore, notwithstanding he swears that he earned more there, besides the salary which their Highnesses gave him, I did not wish to allow more than 50,000 maravedis each year for the work he performs here while he remains here. This I entreat their Highnesses to order allowed to him with the salary from here, and that, because he says and affirms that all the physicians of their Highnesses who are employed in Royal affairs or things similar to this, are accustomed to have by right one day's wages in all the year from all the people. Nevertheless, I have been informed and they tell me, that however this may be, the custom is to give them a certain sum, fixed according to the will and command of their Highnesses in compensation for that day's wages. You will entreat their Highnesses to order provision made as well in the matter of the salary as of this custom, in such manner that the said Dr. Chanca may have reason to be satisfied.

["Their Highnesses are pleased in regard to this matter of Dr. Chanca, and that he shall be paid what the Admiral has assigned him, together with his salary. "In regard to the day's wages of the physicians, they are not accustomed to receive it, save where the King, our Lord, may be in persona.]

"Item. You will say to their Highnesses that Coronel is a man for the service of their Highnesses in many things, and how much service he has rendered up to the present in all the most necessary matters, and the need we feel of him now that he is sick; and that rendering service in such a manner, it is reasonable that he should receive the fruit of his service, not only in future favours, but in his present salary, so that he and those who are here may feel that their service profits them; because, so great is the labour which must be performed here in gathering the gold that the persons who are so diligent are not to be held in small consideration; and as, for his skill, he was provided here by me with the office of Alguacil Mayor of these Indies; and since in the provision the salary is left blank, you will say that I supplicate their Highnesses to order it filled in with as large an amount as they may think right, considering his services, confirming to him the provision I have given him here, and assuring it to him annually.

["Their Highnesses order that 15,000 maravedis more than his salary shall be assigned him each year, and that it shall be paid to him with his salary.]

"In the same manner you will tell their Highnesses how the lawyer Gil Garcia came here for Alcalde Mayor and no salary has been named or assigned to him; and he is a capable person, well educated and diligent, and is very necessary here; that I entreat their Highnesses to order his salary named and assigned, so that he can sustain himself, and that it may be paid from the money allowed for salaries here.

"[Their Highnesses order 20,000 maravedis besides his salary assigned to him each year, as long as he remains yonder, and that it shall be paid him when his salary is paid.]

"Item. You will say to their Highnesses, although it is already written in the letters, that I do not think it will be possible to go to make discoveries this year, until these rivers in which gold is found are placed in the most suitable condition for the service of their Highnesses, as afterwards it can be done much better. Because it is a thing which no one can do without my presence, according to my will or for the service of their Highnesses, however well it may be done, as it is doubtful what will be satisfactory to a man unless he is present.

["Let him endeavour that the amount of this gold may be known as precisely as possible.]

"Item. You will say to their Highnesses that the Squires who came from Granada showed good horses in the review which took place at Seville, and afterward at the embarkation I did not see them because I was slightly unwell, and they replaced them with such horses that the best of them do not appear to be worth 2000 maravedis, as they sold the others and bought these; and this was done in the same way to many people as I very well saw yonder, in the reviews at Seville. It appears that Juan de Soria, after he had been given the money for the wages, for some interest of his own substituted others in place of those I expected to find here, and I found people whom I had never seen. In this matter he was guilty of great wickedness, so that I do not know if I should complain of him alone. On this account, having seen that the expenses of these Squires have been defrayed until now, besides their wages and also wages for their horses, and it is now being done: and they are persons who, when they are sick or when they do not desire to do so, will not allow any use to be made of their horses save by themselves: and their, Highnesses do not desire that these horses should be purchased of them, but that they should be used in the service of their

Highnesses: and it does not appear to them that they should do anything or render any service except on horseback, which at the present time is not much to the purpose: on this account, it seems that it would be better to buy the horses from them, since they are of so little value, and not have these disagreements with them every day. Therefore their Highnesses may determine this as will best serve them.

["Their Highnesses order Don Juan de Fonseca to inform himself in regard to this matter of the horses, and if it shall be found true that this fraud was committed, those persons shall be sent to their Highnesses to be punished: and also he is to inform himself in regard to what is said of the other people, and send the result in the examination to their Highnesses; and in regard to these Squires, their Highnesses command that they remain there and render service, since they belong to the guards and servants of their Highnesses: and their Highnesses order the Squires to give up the horses each time it is necessary and the Admiral orders it, and if the horses receive any injury through others using them, their Highnesses order that the damage shall be paid to them by means of the Admiral.]

"Item. You will say to their Highnesses that more than 200 persons have come here without wages, and there are some of them who render good service. And as it is ordered that the others rendering similar service should be paid: and as for these first three years it would be of great benefit to have 1000 men here to settle, and place this island and the rivers of gold in very great security, and even though there were 100 horsemen nothing would be lost, but rather it seems necessary, although their Highnesses will be able to do without these horsemen until gold is sent: nevertheless, their Highnesses must send to say whether wages shall be paid to these 200 persons, the same as to the others rendering good service, because they are certainly necessary, as I have said in the beginning of this memorandum.

["In regard to these 200 persons, who are here said to have gone without wages, their Highnesses order that they shall take the places of those who went for wages, who have failed or shall fail to fulfil their engagements, if they are skilful and satisfactory to the Admiral. And their Highnesses order the Purser (Contador) to enrol them in place of those who fail to fulfil their engagements, as the Admiral shall instruct him.]

"Item. As the cost of these people can be in some degree lightened and the better part of the expense could be avoided by the same means employed by other Princes in other places: it appears, that it would be well to order brought in the ships, besides the other things which are for the common maintenance and the medicines, shoes and the skins from which to order the shoes made, common shirts and others, jackets, linen, sack-coats, trowsers and cloths suitable for wearing apparel, at reasonable prices: and other things like conserves which are not included in rations and are for the preservation of health, which things all the people here would willingly receive to apply on their wages and if these were purchased yonder in Spain by faithful Ministers who would act for the advantage of their Highnesses, something would be saved. Therefore you will learn the will of their Highnesses about this matter, and if it appears to them to be of benefit to them, then it must be placed in operation.

["This arrangement is to be in abeyance until the Admiral writes more fully, and at another time they will send to order Don Juan de Fonseca with Jimeno de Bribiesca to make provision for the same.]

"Item. You will say to their Highnesses that inasmuch as yesterday in the review people were found who were without arms, which I think happened in part by that exchange which took place yonder in Seville, or in the harbour when those who presented themselves armed were left, and others were taken who gave something to those who made the exchange, it seems that it would be well to order 200 cuirasses sent, and 100 muskets and 100 crossbows, and a large quantity of arsenal supplies, which is what we need most, and all these arms can be given to those who are unarmed.

["Already Don Juan de Fonseca has been written to make provision for this.]

"Item. Inasmuch as some artisans who came here, such as masons and other workmen, are married and have wives yonder in Spain, and would like to have what is owing them from their wages given to their wives or to the persons to whom they will send their requirements in order that they may buy for them the things which they need here I supplicate their Highnesses to order it paid to them, because it is for their benefit to have these persons provided for here.

["Their Highnesses have already sent orders to Don Juan de
Fonseca to make provision for this matter.]

"Item. Because, besides the other things which are asked for there according to the memoranda which you are carrying signed by my hand, for the maintenance of the persons in good health as well as for the sick ones, it would be very well to have fifty casks of molasses (miel de azucar) from the island of Madeira, as it is the best sustenance in the world and the most healthful, and it does not usually cost more than two ducats per cask, without the cask: and if their Highnesses order some caravel to stop there in returning, it can be purchased and also ten cases of sugar, which is very necessary; as this is the best season of the year to obtain it, I say between the present time and the month of April, and to obtain it at a reasonable price. If their Highnesses command it, the order could be given, and it would not be known there for what place it is wanted.

["Let Don Juan de Fonseca make provision for this matter.]

"Item. You will say to their Highnesses that although the rivers contain gold in the quantity related by those who have seen it, yet it is certain that the gold is not engendered in the rivers but rather on the land, the waters of the rivers which flow by the mines bringing it enveloped in the sands: and as among these rivers which have been discovered there are some very large ones, there are others so small that they are fountains rather than rivers, which are not more than two fingers of water in depth, and then the source from which they spring may be found: for this reason not only labourers to gather it in the sand will be profitable, but others to dig for it in the earth, which will be the most particular operation and produce a great quantity. And for this, it will be well for their Highnesses to send labourers, and from among those who work yonder in Spain in the mines of Almaden, that the work may be done in both ways. Although we will not await them here, as with the labourers we have here we hope, with the aid of God, once the people are in good health, to amass a good quantity of gold to be sent on the first caravels which return.

["This will be fully provided for in another manner. In the meantime their Highnesses order Don Yuan de Fonseca to send the best miners he can obtain; and to write to Almaden to have the greatest possible number taken from there and sent.]

"Item. You will entreat their Highnesses very humbly on my part, to consider Villacorta as speedily recommended to them, who, as their Highnesses know, has rendered great service in this business, and with a very good will, and as I know him, he is a diligent person and very devoted to their service: it will be a favour to me if he is given some confidential charge for which he is fitted, and where he can show his desire to serve them and his diligence: and this you will obtain in such a way that Villacorta may know by the result, that what he has done for me when I needed him profits him in this manner.

["It will be done thus.]

"Item. That the said Mosen Pedro and Gaspar and Beltran and others who have remained here gave up the captainship of caravels, which have now returned, and are not receiving wages: but because they are persons who must be employed in

43

important matters and of confidence, their compensation, which must be different from the others, has not been determined. You will entreat their Highnesses on my part to determine what is to be given them each year, or by the month, according to their service.

"Done in the city of Isabella, January 30, 1494.

["This has already been replied to above, but as it is stated in the said item that they enjoy their salary, from the present time their Highnesses order that their wages shall be paid to all of them from the time they left their captainships."]

This document is worth studying, written as it was in circumstances that at one moment looked desperate and at another were all hope. Columbus was struggling manfully with difficulties that were already beginning to be too much for him. The Man from Genoa, with his guiding star of faith in some shore beyond the mist and radiance of the West—see into what strange places and to what strange occupations this star has led him! The blue visionary eyes, given to seeing things immediately beyond the present horizon, must fix themselves on accounts and requisitions, on the needs of idle, aristocratic, grumbling Spaniards; must fix themselves also on that blank void in the bellies of his returning ships, where the gold ought to have been. The letter has its practical side; the requisitions are made with good sense and a grasp of the economic situation; but they have a deeper significance than that. All this talk about little ewe lambs, wine and bacon (better than the last lot, if it please your Highnesses), little yearling calves, and fifty casks of molasses that can be bought a ducat or two cheaper in Madeira in the months of April and May than at any other time or place, is only half real. Columbus fills his Sovereigns' ears with this clamour so that he shall not hear those embarrassing questions that will inevitably be asked about the gold and the spices. He boldly begins his letter with the old story about "indications of spices" and gold "in incredible quantities," with a great deal of "moreover" and "besides," and a bold, pompous, pathetic "I will undertake"; and then he gets away from that subject by wordy deviations, so that to one reading his letter it really might seem as though the true business of the expedition was to provide Coronel, Mosen Pedro, Gaspar, Beltran, Gil Garcia, and the rest of them with work and wages. Everything that occurs to him, great or little, that makes it seem as though things were humming in the new settlement, he stuffs into this document, shovelling words into the empty hulls of the ships, and trying to fill those bottomless pits with a stream of talk. A system of slavery is boldly and bluntly sketched; the writer, in the hurry and stress of the moment, giving to its economic advantages rather greater prominence than to its religious glories. The memorandum, for all its courageous attempt to be very cool and orderly and practical, gives us, if ever a human document did, a picture of a man struggling with an impossible situation which he will not squarely face, like one who should try to dig up the sea-shore and keep his eyes shut the while.

In the royal comments written against the document one seems to trace the hand of Isabella rather than of Ferdinand. Their tone is matter-of-fact, cool, and comforting, like the coolness of a woman's hand placed on a feverish brow. Isabella believed in him; perhaps she read between the lines of this document, and saw, as we can see, how much anxiety and distress were written there; and her comments are steadying and encouraging. He has done well; what he asks is being attended to; their Highnesses are well informed in regard to this and that matter; suitable provision will be made for everything; but let him endeavour that the amount of this gold may be known as precisely as possible. There is no escaping from that. The Admiral (no one knows it better than himself) must make good his dazzling promises, and coin every boastful word into a golden excelente of Spain. Alas! he must no longer write about the lush grasses, the shining rivers, the brightly coloured parrots, the gaudy flies and insects, the little singing birds, and the nights that are like May in Cordova. He must find out about the gold; for it has come to grim business in the Earthly Paradise.

The End